MW01105076

Nightshade

BRENT DREW TOWNSEND

 FriesenPress

Suite 300 - 990 Fort St
Victoria, BC, V8V 3K2
Canada

www.friesenpress.com

ISBN
978-1-5255-3146-0 (Hardcover)
978-1-5255-3147-7 (Paperback)
978-1-5255-3148-4 (eBook)

1. Biography & Autobiography

Distributed to the trade by The Ingram Book Company

Table of Contents

Nightshade

BRENT DREW TOWNSEND

Foreword

Many years have passed since a second-generation homesteader named Graham offered me work on a wild horse ranch in Southern Alberta. At the time, I had just turned twenty. Looking back now, it all seems like a dream.

Prologue
Navaho Blanket

As I stand before the storm, brilliant sunlit patches stream impossibly towards me. Beneath this flowing overcast of sun pocked cloud, bleached beige hillsides reveal a raw wilderness further exposed by time.

The desert produces that *moody light* that only the desert can produce. At once colorful. At once bleak. A monochromatic moonscape, dotted with cactus and sweetened by the over-powering presence of sage.

The cool chocolate waters of this uniquely red river mark the baseline of our Navaho Blanket. Nestled before a pink pastel fringe of river willow and dark cottonwood haunt, these sagebrush embroidered tapestries enclose the much less contrived of cathedrals: the contemptuous coulee. Holding their breath as if eternal, these contorted canyons have long since been silenced by age.

Atop these endless embankments, the slim existence, or non-existence really, of soil producing the morose, mascara-lined mesa' and a scant division of scarified earth that undermines their roots.

Echoing from a chaotic past, a striking cast of shadows routinely invade these brutal labyrinths. Along with the layering of loams that adorn mushroom capped ensembles of cactus and rock. Far below, a maze-like mosaic of muck resembles the interlocking sidewalks of a civilization gone mad.

The Badlands begin as a displaced desert division bordering on madness and defeat. Stretching before us each day, a miniature grand canyon and a vastly timeless plateau of ancient decaying dust. The surviving sediments of exposed sea beds result on scales deceiving to the eyes. Like stepping into the virtual world.

Redcliff

1975

Pounding down the steep river embankment, a pan-
icked herd of feral horses intent on reaching the
other side. Behaving as one, the culmination of several
large outlaw bands now numbering over a thousand,
their motion brutal and brief but streaming deliberately
towards freedom. Out of the sun-crested dunes, into the
dew-damp meadow and across the ruffle-tiered sagebrush plateau, their nostrils flaring, breath visible in the
cold dawn air. A fear-based, primal explosion of enraged
animals taking a seemingly light-speed lead, leaving us too
far behind and out of position to make any difference now.

A rare sight, this seething, amoebic cloak of many
colours, moving in unison and encompassing the fore-
ground like the rolling undulations of a wheat field in the
wind. Far quicker than silver, the leading wave began to
spill over the steep cliff edge and down its banks before
plunging into the sparkling river hundreds of feet below.

The riders—a handpicked assortment of rodeo pros,
arrived in the night in order to infiltrate a known home

1

and favoured breeding ground for summer herds of wild horses. Then, with the element of surprise, they would attempt to drive them out into the open, at which point the trucks would come up from behind and take over by pushing them towards our staging area twenty miles away. But first they had to outwit the wily stallions, who were known to assess a situation for what it was and come up with some very innovative contingency plans of their own.

It wasn't every day you got a call from Graham with the instructions to bring a fast horse, be ready to ride, and if you don't have a "six," you better customize your shotgun in a soft-jawed vice. And Graham knows. This was his idea in the first place; after all, he's the old man, and he was calling the shots. In case anything went wrong, he would be up ahead in his truck, watching from a hilltop. A truck would be no match for a herd in sand anyway, and it would be too noisy, giving away our presence. Nor were these dunes any place for the curious at heart; a chance encounter with an enraged 1,400-pound stallion functioning in seek-and-destroy mode is no laughing matter, even to an armed and experienced rider.

Amidst all the panic and confusion, they can come up on you out of nowhere, and they won't just kill you—they'll kill your horse first, just on principle alone. Then they'll be looking at you, because you smell a little like your horse—and that's a natural threat.

In case you didn't know, a domestic horse's hooves are trimmed for speed and safety, whereas a feral horse has razor-sharp hooves, all roughshod and splinter-chipped from rocks. Hence, being "spiked" with the leading edge of one of these could easily prove fatal, as it will cut you like an axe. Believe me—a wild-eyed stallion protecting his harem is a four-legged warlord with a vengeance for blood.

That said, trucks are rapid, robust, and offer a lot of flexibility—as does a swift saddle horse and a truly adept rider armed with a sawed-off double-barrelled shotgun.

What we learned later on was a little less obvious at the time. With the sun so low, there was a lot of dust and haze obstructing our view. So no one realized we had hit the jackpot, with everyone encountering more horse-power than expected, and then confronting even larger herds further ahead. This sudden infusion of outcast bands, as well as the resulting fusion of numerous dominants, added an extra element of hostility when they all funnelled through into one magnificent melting pot perhaps numbering 1,500. Welcome Hurricane Katrina equestrian-style, and we were in the eye of the storm.

Complete pandemonium took hold, and about all anyone could conclude through that mounting cloud of dust was that, grossly outnumbered, we just lost out. Rallying round, the rival tribes battled fiercely, defended their harems, and made for the wild blue water all at the same time. They were heading for the riverbank, and no one was covering that exit yet.

Time stands still. Silence—like the sullen hush that precedes a rattlesnake's startling serenade—followed instead by the explosive inception of a no-nonsense, matter-of-fact rancher commanding a one-ton truck launched from a high plateau; its tires tracing an invisible path through thin air, with the fugitive red sand wind-milling from spinning hubs.

Time becomes staccato—strobe-like—and loses meaning; horses are whipping the water into a froth, hooves amass in a myriad of mycelium and muck. Breaking this spell, the truck pounds down hard on the earth, bottoming out, its horn blaring loudly and echoing off the cliffs. A plume of dust expelled in all directions rises as evidence of the impact, like some evil dragon's fiery descent—a revving manifestation of industrial ingenuity and mechanical mass in motion intercepting their path. The horses scatter like the parting of the Red Sea as our iron rhino snorts and short-circuits further advances by pinwheeling around several more times in that rising wall of dust.

With horn wailing authority, the rapidly expanding gap between the startled horses spreads in an instant, those escaping down the drop and the remainder—our quarry—now charging towards home. All the outriders conveyed their gut-felt approvals with arm-waving exuberance; half the herd may have escaped, but the sound of six or seven hundred head of horses taking to the wind has its own ambient satisfaction. It was all unfolding just like the old man said: we would race them along the cliff edge.

***

Time passes quickly— it's a blur at best, nightmarish somehow—but now it's over. The pens, six of them, are alive with sweat-soaked, foam-flanked, highly distressed desert hombre, their presence made known by the din and the dust rising a hundred feet into the air, as the sun, ignorant of their pleas, finally worked its way around to the treetops in the west.

Afraid of the Shade

Even in this clear-but-dust-wrought chaos, each moment has a rhythm all its own. Sky-spiralling sparks and billowing smoke roaming slowly throughout this parched, already-arid plain. A macramé of manes, a tangle of tales, a siren-haunted dream world run in reverse. The collective chorus of this least-tamed tempest, continually calling through evening's inevitable, ever-encroaching chill. The silhouettes of stallions attempting to breach corral fences, their shadows seemingly embossed upon the massive cloud hanging over us. A sea of personas—the ebbing, flowing forelock shocks shielding those shifting, anguished eyes. All the while, a glimpse of ourselves returned in their half-hidden, afraid-of-the-shade glare.

Competing for intensity with the soon-to-be setting sun, the cherry-red, forever-fading shades of the branding irons reflected on our faces. Leggy blue-jean cowboys with enormous, disproportionate shadows waving hats and shouting, trying to maintain order. People running in all directions, and then horses—followed by more horses—peeling away in a mad dash, a freight train of manes with a mutual mindset.

Doug comes over to me in a hurry and says, "So, you're getting irons. Well, good, then stay here, where I can find you. But if things start getting a little out of hand, and I kind of think they are, get in a truck . . ."

I said, "Okay," and asked, "when do we let them out?"

Doug chuckled. "Let them out! That's just it—because now it's more a matter of how much longer we're going to be able to keep them in, and not much longer, would be my guess, we just lost one pen. So, if horses start charging through here in all directions—like we just saw down there a few minutes ago—come and get us, fast. That means lay on the horn, drive straight through them if you have to, but get to where we are, and then slide over— we'll know what to do."

"Well, just in case . . ." I asked. "What *would* you do?"

He told me that it wasn't the horses he was concerned with; so getting everybody out of the way would be his priority. He half-joked that he knew he wouldn't like getting jabbed on the tail end with a hot iron either, and if one of those big stallions spots any of us out there, and remembers who did it, he still might be feeling a little put out, you know.

As he walked away, I could hear his voice trailing off, "I don't know why we need so many horses, anyway. One of these is usually more than enough."

For the most part, however, we were successful; we separated the keepers to the better corrals right away—a handful of two year olds and a good number of four year olds. We also succeeded in branding the majority. But when it happened, it happened fast; it was getting near dark when a stretch of fence was defeated, and like water, when one goes, they all flow.

It had been a very long, hot, and dusty day. The time had come to celebrate with a good strong, nerve-steadying snort. We decided to move into an abandoned shack that had once belonged to Alan. Although it hadn't been occupied since he died, we all knew he would have liked it this way, and nobody had to remove their boots.

We spread ourselves around in the largest of several rooms. Further complementing an already-filthy floor, the rusty, corroding kitchen chairs with torn backs and worn-out seats were quite inviting. Dusty, personified apparel, all present and accounted for, each item collectively indicating everyone's exhaustion and pride: hats, chaps, spurs, Storm Riders, and discarded leather gloves lying about, looking as wrinkled as our shadowy five o'clock faces.

The receiving party was ready for us. Rose had instructed the younger girls not to bother with anything unnecessary, such as folding cloth napkins or providing cups, cutlery, or even plates. She just wanted to make sure the food didn't run out. This was an interesting still life, if ever I saw one: the ranch women with trays; Graham, seated front and centre with an entire case of whiskey by his side, handing out bottles here and there, each one promptly twisted open, tilted upright, and gurgling with more gusto than a busy office water cooler.

The room was relatively smoke-free; whereas healthy, three-fingered pinches of snoose plucked from cans of chewing tobacco were in high demand until the food arrived. The girls continued to retrieve empty sandwich trays, replacing them with several well-appointed cold cut arrangements, including pickles, cheese, and crackers, along with entire rings of salami. They commended us on a very successful day before vanishing from sight.

Having flushed the dust from our throats, the comments began to surface. A darkened figure across from me suggested that it would be a good time to discuss what had happened. "First of all," he said, "how did we wind up with that many horses? And what's more, that was not normal horse behaviour. That herd lit up like the Fourth of July."

Nods were going around the room faster than firewater; he was right, the horses had been panic-stricken, and just like he said, there hadn't been any small, loner bands like we had expected to see. Everyone had been in charge of a surprisingly large herd with no help in sight. So they had all been wondering: *Where is everybody?* When, instead of going with them, another rider behind an equally large band appeared, moving towards them. Then, just as they were both starting to say, "Well, don't bring them over here!" several more large groups of horses began pouring in right on top of them. And that's when everything went sour enough to curdle your blood.

This was by no means what anyone had anticipated. Not only that, but a handful of riders shouldn't elicit a massive cliff-side escape. The normal, more general trend should include the herd initially *trotting*—possibly even *walking*—away in the opposite direction. This was the kind of "squeeze play" we had in mind: cool, calm, and collected.

It isn't until you're nearing the pens that you need to get a little ahead of their thinking. Then it's okay to pick up the pace. They need to see everything as an escape route—not a trap.

Graham commented that since the military base we were on, didn't like the herds and wanted them removed, that might explain why the stallions had been so frantic. By gaining permission to enter the restricted zone in advance, he had tipped off the higher-ranking officials, who probably thought they'd be doing us as big a favour as we were doing them.

We had no way of knowing, however, the horses may have been confined to the same area and intimidated for days; in other words, whirly birds.

Then we snuck in beneath dawn's early light, and that really set things off.

It wasn't until then that we got around to the question of: Did anyone see Pat?

***

I didn't really know Pat, but Pat was about as cowboy as cowboy gets, and he liked to ride bulls. Pat was suited to rodeo-life as well as living on the range; he was tough, knowledgeable, gutsy, never spoke, and had piercing eyes.

Frankly, he unnerved me somewhat, with his intense, almost-military demeanour.

Pat rode a big black stallion that he alone favoured, undoubtedly because he was the only one who could get near it. Much more, stay on it. Much less, reach that high stirrup, should anyone be fool enough to try. Like Pat it was tall business, and with those legs, it could really eat up the ground. They were both in top physical condition.

"Pat! Is he here?" It was Graham's voice, heard again through the encroaching dark. We all fell silent until someone volunteered that they saw Pat earlier on, and he passed them like a shot on that big black stud he always rides.

He continued, saying that it looked like he was having a little trouble, because his horse, having caught wind of all those brood mares, was starting to entertain a few ideas of its own, and I doubt they included having Pat around, particularly on its back.

He added that Pat took the lead with some of the fastest outlaws in the bunch; he had both feet on the dashboard and was hauling back on the steering column for all he was worth when his bridal snapped, and he was last seen thundering down a steep embankment with one of the more radical splinter groups, destination unknown.

In light of the seriousness of the situation, only a few of us chuckled. As far as we knew, he could have had a run-in with a pissed-off stallion and was seriously hurt.

His not having a bit and bridal would make the outcome a little more challenging.

All told, everybody witnessed an incredible, chance-in-a-lifetime event, and although we nearly lost the entire lot to the river, we were spared by Graham's decisive actions. So everything went according to plan, nobody got hurt, and everyone received an incredible gift from the old man: a snorting, full-of-spunk, four-year-old bronc.

The Range

Graham's Horse

It always makes me laugh when I'm told that something "inanimate" has a mind of its own. Many is the time I've heard such remarks regarding a fast motorbike, snowboard or racing skis. While personifying a lifeless object may have merit, watching a bucking horse twist its head around to look you in the eye prior to piling you in a cactus patch is far more provocative.

Because the majority of horses we had on the ranch were wild, very few of them could be recognized as user friendly. They were all outlaws at heart and couldn't be toyed with. Although I had numerous memorable experiences on Graham's cattle horse, Red, they were never what I would call "relaxing." To this day, I can recall being terrorized by both the animal's speed and disposition. You know, it's not easy to feather the reins when you're certain you're going to die.

Just thinking I could handle Red was a big mistake because he was obviously a one-man horse. Then, because he refused to walk, I hauled back on the reins and didn't release them. Pulling on the reins needlessly is a little like stepping on someone's toes; you are asking for trouble, and Red went awry. Seldom are the times when I've moved over rough ground with such reckless abandon.

I knew I was in for it when we entered a narrow coulee with a creek running through it. Weaving side to side slalom-style, we leapt across the muddy banks, scraping past low limbs and thorny bushes. Since I was still on, Red decided to climb a steep incline instead. So steep that he stunned himself when his head slammed into the clay bank, causing him to collapse beneath me with a long, agonizing moan.

The moment my feet hit the ground, I dismounted so he wouldn't roll onto me. Then I stood over him, contemplating my existence. Well, I don't know if I was long on guts or short on brains—maybe both, but I didn't want to walk, so just as he was attempting to stand, I jumped back on.

Rising on all fours, he returned a look of disdain, and took off again. It seemed that Red was still intent on killing me, or worse. Having gained the flat top, Red's next ploy was to scare the daylights out of me by charging full speed towards the cliff. Then, at the last possible moment, he stopped, presumably while I continued beyond the ledge.

I thought that we were going over, so I gripped the horn with both hands, to prevent myself from plummeting into a cactus-bottomed abyss—something I'm certain Red would have gotten quite a kick out of.

Never let it be said that horses don't have a sense of humour. They do.

He charged the cliff repeatedly, each time sitting down like a dog to maximize his stopping power. However, he probably got a few cactus spines in his rump doing that, so, he bolted away in the opposite direction instead.

You know the rhythm a galloping horse makes as its hooves trample the ground? Well at this speed, it sounded like the audio was on fast forward. Believe me, we were on fire. Unfortunately, this incredible pattering of hooves stopped abruptly, as something neither Red nor I were prepared for, a hidden three-foot drop, left us without a leg to stand on. Slamming down on the ground, Red stumbled badly, tossing me out of the saddle. I nearly knocked myself out, smacking my head on his solid cranium. However, I landed on my back, looking skyward, only to see an upside-down horse perform an aerial flip above me. While I didn't see him touch down, I gathered that we were both pretty beat up.

Red recovered first; then I got up in a completely dazed state and walked several feet, noticing that we had both landed in the only patch of prairie not covered in prickly pear. On the verge of collapse, I returned to that cacti-free zone and lay back down. My entire body was throbbing.

I got up eventually, and the saddle looked okay, so I crawled back on Red, who was calmly standing by. From here, he walked me back to the barn, where everyone was relieved to see us.

The first words I heard from Graham's eldest son, Terry, were: "What happened, Brent?"

"Red took a bad fall and landed hard," I replied.

"Okay, we'll check him out—you better go sack-out for a while."

So I did.

I learned later on that Red's back was swollen, and that his "bars" looked bruised; the bars refer to a space in a horse's mouth where the bit rests. That's the communication center.

It was the very next day that Doug and I were in a 4 x 4 up on the hilltop when I recognized a certain cliff edge and said, "Hey, this is where Red was trying to toss me off the cliff."

Doug said, "What?" He was staring at me with a look of concern. Although he had heard a little from the others about my unplanned excursion, Doug had been away in town at the time, and it wasn't until now that he insisted on full disclosure. So, I briefly described the episode.

Doug said, "You mean Red was performing slides on the cliff edge?"

"Yeah, but I knew he'd never go through with it. Just the same," I added, "I'll bet he was stopping about a foot from the drop." Then I reconsidered my remark as highly exaggerative, and stated that it was probably a lot further back than that, and that it had just *seemed* worse while looking down from the saddle. With this, Doug stopped the truck and got out to see how far I would have been thrown.

I was right; this was exactly where we had been, and Doug and I did in fact find skid marks in the clay. The distance Red's front hooves stopped before the edge was about a foot—maybe sixteen inches, no more.

Doug looked at me in disbelief. He said, "If I was on a horse like Red and it was charging towards a cliff, I'd be thinking about getting off a lot further back than this; that horse is crazy." Following with, "I don't know why Dad likes that horse so much. He should get rid of it before somebody gets killed."

During the few other times I had to ride Red, I was extremely light on the reins—feather light—and he was more tolerant.

The Sandman
Horses can't talk, but they listen.

The man from the stockyard was a real hotshot; you could tell by his tailored suit and matching hat.

"Why don't you get yourself a true 'cattle-working' horse, and not some big lumbering monster like that? You'll get way more work out of a smaller, fleet-footed horse than you will with a bigger animal that you don't need in the first place. Now, you look at *my* horse—she's not big, but I'm not roping. I'm penning cattle, that truck is waiting, and I want it done fast!"

We watched as his horse, Little Lena, attempted to keep a safe distance from the bulls. Spurs flashed occasionally, betraying her wisdom, as they pried and raked each time her reluctance became apparent.

The next thing we knew, they were both on the ground. The rider was taken totally by surprise. What started out okay soon went wrong when a big exotic bull launched them into the air. The sudden compression was so violent that it broke the horse's back in an instant.

This all happened on an entirely different ranch that was owned by a gentleman I only knew as Sandy. Sandy was more than what anyone would regard as a superb horseman; he was clearly a master, and he kept some very expensive bulls. Atop of his impressive horse, he got the job done with so much expertise that they moved more out of reaction than threat, causing me to wonder if he was some kind of matador.

Sandy was extremely formidable in stature, and as a major land baron, the word I got was that he was in fact a crown prince. Furthermore, I understood that he was a hard man, and not especially easy to work with. So, in spite of his generous offer to stay on as one of the hands, I turned him down by defining my previous commitments at home.

Well, our decked-out cattleman from the city wasn't entirely on his feet when he clued in to our calls to "Get clear!" Then, seeing the bull's fixed gaze, he returned a look of stark terror, and that's when he was vaulted skyward again; but this time it was the "Sandman" who hauled him across the back of his own horse with one hand, piling him on the far side of the corral fence before he really knew what had hit him.

Then, as he rode away, we heard Sandy say, "How do you like your little horses now?"

Teamwork

Venom!

The little girl's squeals were anything but delight. She was only five, and as a preschooler she had accompanied us on one of our more casual routines. Today we were berry picking.

Along with her screams came the word "snake," and as I looked down, I could see what she meant. An extremely large and aggressive bull snake, rivalling the size of a small boa, was attempting to breach the truck box, by propping itself over the large tires of our 4 x 4.

We had only just arrived, and typical of our cause we had backed up to the tall Saskatoon bushes and climbed into the back. I was only beginning to climb up a stepladder to pick from the top limbs when the fuss began.

Of secondary nature, our truck box platform did in fact offer very good protection from the snakes that were common along the riverbanks this time of year. The Badlands weren't termed as such without reason. This arid cacti-strewn plain was home to numerous oddities, including rattlesnakes, bull snakes, black widow spiders, horned toads, and scorpions, too. Horned toads and scorpions were extremely rare, whereas the pit vipers and non-venomous (but far more aggressive) bull snakes were common. We would regularly see rattlers warming themselves on the road, and I once had to remain on a stepladder I was using to trim a hedge because one had parked itself at the bottom.

Bull snakes could occasionally be seen making the rounds in the barn as they searched for mice, and I saw one close up (which I estimated to be eight feet long) slowly leaving our garden, having just scared the daylights out of a small child riding his tricycle nearby.

The one currently pitching its body against the side of our truck with resounding thumps was a bit bigger than that—and man, was it mad. Not only that, it was nearly inside!

The next thing I knew was that its head—roughly the size of your fist—flew a good ten feet in the opposite direction following the hollow, metallic *clunk* of a garden hoe. The snake had been neatly cleaved in two.

Looking down, I could see the immense body writhing around like the spinning carriage of an old push lawnmower.

It all happened so fast that I didn't really have time to react, but I was glad Graham did. Seeing that his granddaughter was all right, he set down the hoe and swung himself out of the box and right into the driver's seat without touching the ground. "We may have driven over its tail," he said, offering a possible explanation for the seemingly unprovoked attack. He then advised us to "hold on," as we were going to move to another grove, adding, "He might have friends."

A Good Horse Is Never a Bad Colour (Unless It's Hurt)

I can't remember if the drink ever touched my lips or not, but I doubt it. "Two and a red" was what we had ordered. In other words, six glasses in total: we both had two draughts and a glass of tomato juice to blend. It might sound odd if you don't know what I'm talking about, but it makes for a nice refreshing drink, especially in the afternoon when you don't want too much of a glow showing.

What I recall was that the waitress was beginning to set the drinks down when someone standing in the door of the tavern shouted, "Who owns the green 4 x 4 with the stock trailer?" He was looking our way.

Graham slammed me on the shoulder and said, "That sounds like us!" Then he stood and addressed the stranger as to why.

The stranger in turn began to explain that a "kid" had picked up the electric cattle prod from the back of the truck and used it on the bull, jolting it in the bag several times. The bull had reacted by crashing through the internal divider and was now taking out his rage on our horse.

33

Adding that the kid was long gone, he said, "That bull is going to kill your horse!"

A crowd was gathering outside, but they were keeping a safe distance as our trailer rocked side to side, sometimes seeming to leave the ground. The horse was totally defenseless and kept tripping over the downed latticework of the metal divider. If it weren't for the fact that the bull was polled (meaning, it didn't have horns), the horse would have suffered beyond description and probably bled to death in a matter of minutes. Still, I was shocked by the Charolais' raw strength. He would side check the horse time and time again. Then, whenever he had it cornered, he would place his muscular neck beneath the horse's girth and toss the 1,200-pound animal into the air with a simple flick. More than once I watched the horse slam against the trailer's low ceiling.

The bull marched up and down like a reigning "prize fighter," and whenever his field of view included our horse, that old cow pony got hell just for being there.

"Get in!" was all Graham said.

We were probably in motion before I was seated, and we left in a hurry. However, the bull wasn't done yet, and our one-ton swayed as we sped through town; just keeping the vehicle in the intended lane took some effort. That's when we could hear a car horn honking. Graham looked over to me and said, "There's a car coming up from behind—I think he wants to tell us we have a problem."

This proved to be true, as the car crossed the centerline, facing head-on traffic, and pulled up alongside. The passenger was waving madly and shouting, "Hey! Hey!" He kept pointing at our trailer.

Graham glanced over to me and said, "It's as if we don't know." Then shouted back to them, "Want me to unload him here?"

With that, the car's passenger immediately realized his ignorance and slapped the driver on the shoulder, indicating to him to fall back. That was the last we saw of them. Besides, we had problems of our own as we careened through an otherwise-quiet residential area.

Graham told me he knew a few ranchers on the outskirts of town who would probably understand if we unloaded our livestock in their field. However, it wasn't long before that bull quieted down, possibly due to the presence of a steady breeze coursing through the trailer. So, as urgent as our situation was, we continued the rest of the way home instead, and the minute we got through our entrance gate, we stopped. Graham had advised me to get up on the truck where I would be safe; he in turn did what was needed, even though he was placing himself in harm's way by approaching the rear of the trailer and swinging the gate wide open. The bull was the first to exit, and it trotted away to investigate its new surroundings. Then the horse stepped down awkwardly from the trailer. There were tears in Graham's eyes as he spoke softly to his horse; "Sorry" was all he said.

Our rudely interrupted day was the topic of conversation around the dinner table that night. As usual, Graham was on the phone making business calls and future plans. Graham used to supply the Calgary Stampede with all their "bucking stock"—that is, wild horses from the block—so he knew all the managers. He was talking to one while I sat by and listened.

He told the gentleman that he had a bull he thought might be worthy of rodeo life, commenting that this one was "pretty snuffy." I gathered that the Stampede board representative was somewhat reluctant as rodeo stock is generally quite expensive. Furthermore, this was an unproven animal as far as rodeo events are concerned.

Graham explained that it was actually a mutual favour he had in mind. All he wanted was what the bull would bring if he put it up for sale in the auction, and not celebrity dollars. He was intent on selling this animal as soon as possible, and he just thought they might benefit from a bull of this temperament. It was simply an educated guess. However, he added in no uncertain terms, "We don't want him here."

So the deal was struck, and this way that bull—primarily a victim of circumstance—wouldn't be dealt a death sentence. We had a cattle liner pick him up the very next day.

So how did this all happen? To recap, the field in which we had kept that animal was practically in view of the ranch house. However, the South Saskatchewan River ran deep and wide that time of year, and the only bridge available to us was in Medicine Hat. Graham was more than aware that it was illegal to load a bull with a horse in the same trailer; however, as he pointed out, we had a divider and the bull was polled. Not only that, but prior to this we hadn't had any trouble with this particular animal.

Our entire motive was to save gas and time. Now that we had already driven one hundred miles just to get across the river, it was a long way back to the ranch house. Had we have taken the horse and bull separately (like we should have), that would have meant—three trips instead of one.

Our second more revealing error in judgment occurred when we stopped in town for refreshments; that's where the real trouble began. I never mentioned this to Graham, but in retrospect, I had to wonder about the description of the "kid" who riled the bull up in the first place. To me it seemed improbable that a schoolboy would recognize

our cattle prod for what it was. I also thought it provocative that the man who entered the bar to alert us to the
problem knew exactly where to find us, even though we
were parked on the street and not in the tavern's parking
lot. In essence, he seemed far more likely to have worked
with cattle and electric prods; he knew the terminology of
"stock trailer," and may even have been familiar with the
regulations. In my opinion, he had had an agenda of his
own, which involved purposely causing both the bull and
our saddle horse undue trauma.

Lynx

Double Suspension!

Cheetahs, as most people know, hold the world record for the fastest land animal, with their running bursts approaching 70 mph.

Topping out at around 43 mph, the greyhound is considered to be amongst the fastest of dog breeds. However, the two have something else in common; they both exhibit a double-suspension gallop (although this isn't easily noticed or defined— I'll get there).

Anyway, the less commonly known pronghorn antelope, native to Southern Alberta, are North America's fastest land animal. If need be, they are capable of sustained speeds of over 50 mph. Endangered as these oddities are, we would still see both large and small bands of them around the ranch. In my opinion, they're rather homely looking, being all "cucumber and hooves." Something else we had on the ranch was a greyhound that Terry rescued from the racetrack.

Where we were going or what we were doing, I don't recall, but the dog jumped out of the truck we were in, then took off in the opposite direction. Calling her did no good, and that pup vanished into a plume of dust. So we finally got to see what a double-suspension gallop meant.

What we ourselves didn't notice until then was that there were a half-dozen pronghorn out on the open range. That greyhound probably had never seen any of these creatures before, and they really piqued her curiosity.

Her hind legs "snapped" out from under her with incredible precision, then seemed to trail motionless, and she was completely off the ground. Then one forepaw swept past, tucking beneath her slender ribcage, and again she took flight. Finally, the remaining forepaw followed through, just as the hinds sprung forward, neatly taking the lead by a nose, and the cycle repeated.

Hence, the dog was fully suspended, not once—as is the case with a galloping horse that uses both forelegs simultaneously—but twice, with this one-two-three rhythm. All we could do was watch. As soon as the pronghorn knew they had company, they began to put a little distance between themselves and the inquisitive greyhound—or so they thought. They undoubtedly identified this private investigator as "K9 Class"—in other words, no real threat—and they weren't paying much attention as they shifted into second gear, with their heads up as they proudly bounded away.

Picture the Silver Bullet Express closing in on a slow-moving freight, followed by a near rear-end collision. Or, as Graham put it, "She got close enough to blow some snot up their butts," because it did look like a nip took place.

Those antelope were alarmed, because no coyote they'd ever known could catch them alive, and now it seemed more like aliens had just landed. It was clear that they were scared out of their wits, because they kicked it down into overdrive and left that dog behind like it was standing still. We all learned a "quick" lesson that day, and I would be surprised if those particular antelope ever returned to that corner of the field again.

Punchline!

Graham wasn't in the least impressed. It wasn't so much that supper was late; it was the circumstances surrounding it that had him on the phone to the RCMP. Several of the ranch women (both his wife, Rose, and their daughter-in-law, Bonnie) had done some shopping in town and were making their way home, only to be held up by the workers at a large plant on the outskirts.

Graham didn't exactly own the road—not all of it anyway. His father, Alan had settled there before Redcliff was even on the map, and he created the road, including the portion that was right on their land just by going to town. That fact still didn't put Graham in charge—but then again, from what I had seen of his demeanour, I wouldn't want to push the point.

Anyway, the plant workers had discovered what they deemed harmless amusement. Leaving work, they would "run" a stop sign and parade bumper to bumper onto a secondary highway, and this way, they could delay travellers until all four or five hundred cars were on their way.

Another point of contention was that they gestured rudely and catcalled the ladies for no reason, embarrassing them and making them feel quite uncomfortable. I was still in the kitchen and sitting at the table when Graham became a bit short with whomever he was discussing the matter with on the phone. Apparently, the constable had indicated that he "couldn't and wouldn't do anything about it."

Graham hung up the phone, stating, "Then I might."

He had already suggested that the police were all too willing to pull him over and run a siphon line down his tank in the event that Graham was driving a farm vehicle to town, when the regulations state that purple gas was restricted to farm use. Graham said, "You'll do that, but you refuse to go out to this plant and issue traffic tickets for running a stop sign, ignoring the right of way, and endangering lives on a major thoroughfare, times five hundred?"

Following that, he went into the other room and probably watched some television. I went home and turned in; it had been a long day, and I was feeling a little tired. My mornings on the ranch always started early. Graham and I would have breakfast together, and so would the dogs. Then came our daily chores, which were always a rigorous workout. Afterwards, we always had some kind of an interest to pursue, be it handling cattle or farming, which included repairing machinery, or perhaps mending fences or building something.

Today was a little different, because we needed some materials in town and Graham said he wanted me to accompany him. So I did. We got all that done, and we even had time to stop for "two and a red" at the tavern. Still, it was a hot day; I was drowsy, as could be expected with a couple of drinks in me, and I think I was nodding off while leaving the responsibility of driving up to him.

We were nearly home when Graham poked me on the shoulder, waking me up. He said he could see someone parked across the road up ahead, and although he seemed to be moving slowly, he wasn't exactly in a hurry to get clear of the oncoming traffic. We were almost at the parking entrance of the plant, and though I had long forgotten the problems Bonnie and Rose had described, it all came rushing back into my mind. The jokesters were up to their tricks again.

Numerous vehicles were passing us in the oncoming lane, yet a tight "S" bend of two or three vehicles completely obstructing the way loomed before us. They had opted to stop and make a nuisance of themselves. However, this time it wasn't a couple of girls in a sedan; it was the anvil-fisted Graham, and we were in a heavy-duty one-ton 4 x 4 doing 60 mph.

"You better put on your safety belt," Graham said to me, continuing that we might not be able to stop in time. He added that we had the right of way anyhow. While I was in the action of buckling up, Graham commented that the thing they don't seem to understand is that *they're* the ones who are going to get hit!

Just the sound of truck tires on pavement in an otherwise silent cab; I could now see the workers having the time of their lives, laughing it up in the car. Apparently, they envisioned themselves as the celebrities of the lunchroom, much the same as whoever held up our women the day before were. They were making faces and gesturing with their fingers. From where I sat, it looked like half a peace sign, so I wasn't sure if that was a good or a bad thing. But their expressions soon turned to sheer panic when they realized we weren't braking. Now they were pointing at us, and their jaws were going slack! We could see the whites of their eyes, and they could see ours.

Graham shrugged.

Horns were blaring as they prompted the cars in front of them to get out of the way. However, their roadblock was a little too effective for that, and I watched two fast-back sedans hit the ditch as we sped through, narrowly missing them.

"Don't look back," Graham instructed me. "Well, maybe once."

So I did.

***

Well, the trip home was pretty quiet, allowing me a little time to weigh the entire scenario over in my mind, including the unexpected trip to town. The last thing I recall asking Graham was, "Wouldn't we have gotten hurt?"

Graham shook his head, saying, "It's sort of like when you punch someone . . . although it may hurt your fist, it won't hurt nearly as much as how your fist hurts *them*."

We never had any more trouble at that intersection again.

Conversations with Jacob

The kitchen in my Grandfather's house was dimly lit. We sat across from each other, the only thing between us a bottle of whiskey, two glasses, and a can of 7 Up. The curtains remained drawn, but sparrows and wrens cast their shadows upon them as they swooped and snatched the grain and crumbs he had put out that morning.

"Vell," he said, "Now ve is going to have a drink," and he put so much rye in my glass that there was no room to add mix. Wetting his whistle, he let out a sigh and again began to speak. He had a habit of repeating himself and spoke often of how he wound up in Turkey. "Water was *su*, and wine, they called *şarap*. Their bread was known as *ekmek*."

There was a twinkle in his one good eye as he paused, and raised his glass to sip the sweet whiskey I had purchased for the event. I raised my glass too, and tears swarmed to my eyes as the hot stuff burned to my belly.

"Water was *su*, wine *şarap*, bread *ekmek*. That was a long time ago."

Before I knew it, I was experiencing the Russian Revolution. The thunder of hooves, the clashing of steel sabres, pistol shots, rifle reports, and Gatling guns too. He spoke of Cossacks, and one named "Martin" who rode like the wind, deserting him and several others when a river fording they attempted was fouled by "Reds" who lay waiting in a sandbagged machine-gun nest.

All were pinned down on the bank, while the slow, steady repeating rifle worked them over. Martin escaped, draping himself low on the horse's side opposite the gun. Those who remained lay behind wounded, writhing horses—until the deafening sound of the gun suddenly stopped.

The gunners were busy defending their nest; they didn't hear the horse approaching from behind. The first man was trampled, and the second beheaded by Martin's sabre. He returned to the others with horses belonging to the Red Army, and together, they slipped into the night.

CPSIA information can be obtained
at www.ICGtesting.com
Printed in the USA
LVHW010857171118
597429LV00003B/3/P

9 781525 531477